Bringing Your Vision to Life

Why Wait - Be Great!

By: Jasmine Phipps

Dedication

I lost my Auntie Gina Estrada recently due to cancer and I am dedicating this book to her. She was one of the strongest women I knew, not only was she a fighter but she wrote a best-selling book about how to overcome the struggles of cancer as she was battling her own. If you were lucky enough to be blessed with her presence in your life then you know she was one of those people that could change your life with just one conversation. She inspired many, with her kind heartedness, selflessness, and pure, loving nature. She is on my list as one of the greats, next to Kobe, Michael, Flo Jo, because not only did she touch me in many ways she touched thousands of people and she changed the world with the circumstances she was given. She is the definition of greatness and how to achieve greatness yourself.

Foreword

As an adult, we often forget the challenges of growing up - the pain that comes with the feeling of not belonging, the sadness of feeling that you are not being seen for who you are, and the heaviness and fear that these feelings will never end.

As adults, although we know these experiences will end, we are sometimes at a loss for how-to effectively support the young people in our lives. This book is not only a gift to young people, it is an invaluable tool for parents, aunts, uncles, teachers and any other adults who have children in their lives.

Jasmine bravely reveals the pain of being bullied at a school she had been attending since Kindergarten. She shares the pain of her first betrayal and learning the lesson that people are not always who they portray themselves to be. Jasmine shows us how to deal with these slights and find inner-strength to get in touch with our capacity to love and value ourselves as we are. The words on these pages reflect the hard work of one young woman and the love and support of caring parents.

There were many ways that Jasmine's story could have unfolded: she could have sunk into despair, engaged in unhealthy behaviors, or given up on excelling in academics or working to become a track star. Instead, Jasmine discovered the solace that can come from putting your thoughts down on paper -- which resulted in this book.

As there is no age limit to Jasmine's experiences, some adults may find that this book speaks to them through all stages of life.

Inca Mohamed

Table of Contents

Find Me Online!

I will send you updates about everything that is happening. The next book will be about my college life but until then make sure to listen in on my podcast called Spilling Tea with a POC to get weekly updates on my college life.

Website: Jasminephipps.com
Link Tree: linktr.ee/jasminephipps
Follow my Personal Instagram: @jasmine_phipps
Follow my Podcast Instagram: @spillingteawithapoc

Register your Book!

jasminephipps.com/be-great

Introduction

ABOUT ME

My name is Jasmine Phipps, I am the author of this book. I started writing this book at the age of 16, but when I was 11 years old, I had a vision that I was going to change the world. I started writing speeches at around the same time. When I was 11 I never thought in a million years that I was going to be able to become a published author let alone be able to even start to write a book. But through the obstacles that I overcame, I learned that anything you can imagine is achievable, so whatever you want out of life is possible. Everyone is writing their own success story, some don't know it, whereas some do. In the end, the only thing that matters is, will it be worth reading, in our eyes.
Sometimes you have to think if I went into a library right now and read a book about my life would I be proud of how everything turned out?

If not, then you are reading the right book. I want to become a motivational speaker, but I didn't always want to do that–it was my passion to help people that led me to my purpose. I have learned that my purpose on this earth is to help motivate my generation.

THE CARDEN YEARS

My story started at Carden School of Fresno, a little private school that goes from junior kindergarten through eighth grade. I started as a kindergartener and stayed all the way through the eighth grade. Carden was the only school I had gone to my whole life, before high school, and it is where I began to develop an idea of who Jasmine Phipps was.

When I began 2nd grade, I was diagnosed with attention deficit hyperactivity disorder (ADHD). A lot of people at my school didn't know I had ADHD because I kept it a secret. I thought having ADHD was embarrassing and the label DISORDER made me feel like it was something that I should be ashamed of. I learned that ADHD can be an advantage when you learn how to take control of it but I didn't always see it like that. When I learned how to navigate life with ADHD, I started figuring out what strengths came with it and began to work from there to build a foundation where it became a strength rather than weakness.

I had problems with reading until the third grade and I was often embarrassed because I felt like a "dumb kid". I really wasn't able to understand, at the time, how growing up with ADHD could be an advantage. The only thing I remembered was that I would always finish my work the fastest and be scolded because of it. My brain moved so fast at times while the class would move slow. My mind would often adrift from the class material and it became difficult to focus. Therefore, I would often be in the slower learning groups since I could not focus.

When I learned how to control the obstacles placed in front of me, I was able to learn how to use ADHD to my advantage. We often let the world or other people's opinions control our life, but it is when you learn to take control you actually start living. The only one who can define our lives is us.

The only thing I felt I was good at was math. This little private school I went to, made sure we all knew who were the smartest kids in the class. I am grateful that my parents decided to get me help. While working an extra 2 hours after school, I was now on track with the rest of the class. Mind you, I was 7 and we are just getting started with my story.

BEING THE YOUNGEST

I've always been the youngest in my class because my dad put me in kindergarten when I was four years old. Carden put me in an environment where I always had to work hard to prove myself. They made learning a competition. In fourth grade I remember that we would learn our lessons in groups. Our class had only 12 students. There were three groups, so each group had four students. The groups were divided by how smart the teacher thought we were at the beginning of the school year and as the quarters went on you could either get moved up or down.

The first group was the talented and smart kids, the second group was smart but had to work a little harder and the third group struggled the most. The third group included kids who didn't know how to use their strengths and they often needed the most help. Initially, I was in the last group for reading and the second group for math. I remember my goal was to get moved up all the way to the first group for both subjects.

In the second quarter of fourth grade I was moved up only in the math group. I was happy but I still wanted more in order to demonstrate my full strength. I wanted to be moved up in the reading group. I had my mind set that I wasn't going to stop until I accomplished my goal.

I didn't really get better at reading until I was in the 6th and 7th grade. But it was because I made the decision to get better, and acted upon it, that I succeeded. I was taught that the only way to make a weakness better is to keep on improving it until it becomes a strength. I started by reading more books that I was interested in which led me to read all the African American books in our library at school. It took me ten years to see how those groups were really life lessons God was trying to teach me. In life I realized there are always three groups: first group, people who are overachievers; second group, people with skill and talent but need to work to get to the next group by fostering their skills; and the third group is people who need help but decide to settle. I, just like everyone else in the third group, always had a chance to reach the first group. It just was a matter of making the choice to put in the work to do so. Life is never really fair, however, if you put in the work you can move from one group to another, and learn from your failures or you can just stay where you are.

Carden taught me many life lessons, through various challenges, but because of the foundation from Carden, high school was easier for me academically. I wanna give a shoutout to my eighth grade English teacher, Mr. Blanks because he taught me not only how to write but how to express myself through writing. Self-expression is very important because it allows you to be confident not only in writing but in who you are as a person and helps with personal development. I learned life lessons in his class no matter what we were talking about.

As I grew up, my plans for my future became more crystallized. For the longest time I wanted to go to the Olympics and to be the fastest person that ever lived. I've always set my goals pretty high. The first time I told my mom I wanted to go to the Olympics, I was 7 years old. I had seen another little black girl who looked just like me, named Gabby Douglas, compete in the Olympics and win a gold medal for gymnastics. I told my mom I want to be just like her, I wanted to inspire other black girls.

My drive for success definitely comes from being raised by two successful parents who showed me that anything was possible. But what drives me more is understanding why it is so important that I keep going until I fulfill the goals I have set for myself because I don't want to wake up one day and regret my life, regret not doing something when I was fully capable. I don't want to wake up one day knowing there was more I could've done if only I stuck with it a little longer. There is a very famous meme where there are two guys, one who gave up but only had to dig a little deeper to get to the diamonds and another who didn't stop trying and got to it. I will not feel accomplished until I physically know there is nothing more I could do. When you reach that point in life you, your mentally state changes. The little things that you once felt are holding you back don't matter because you see the bigger picture: the long term goal.

TRACK AND FIELD

I started track in third grade. I remember out of all my friends I was the only one who qualified for the next meet. That's where my track story starts. My parents always knew I was an athlete. A lot of my family members were athletes. I played every sport I was able to. I liked playing with the boys because they were always more competitive. I've always been competitive at whatever I did. I wanted to be the best in anything I took on.

From the age of three, as long as Jan Thomas swim school would take me, my parents enrolled me in swimming lessons.

I can only imagine how much money they spent there. One of my swimming coaches said I could have continued swimming and competed at the olympic level and he saw that in me at the age of 5. But when I turned 6 years old, I started playing other sports and gradually stopped swimming. I found a love for running. Running became my place to escape from the pressures of the real world; I was able to free my mind. It was a place where I could be me without getting in trouble for all the uncontrolled energy I had. I loved competing and going to practice. Competing is second nature for me. I ran track, alongside playing volleyball and basketball, all the way through the 8th grade. But after 8th grade I decided to devote all my time to track because my coach told me that I needed to focus on track in order to get to the next level.

In high school I saw a lot of people play a sport and you would think they wouldn't let anyone come between them and that sport, but let their coaches or other adults change how they felt about it. Although I have a love/hate relationship with track, it is my passion and the love I have for it that won't let me stop doing it. Nobody in this world can change how I feel about track but me. The few coaches I've had that didn't believe in me didn't make me stop loving it but instead made me want it more. No one should be able to change how we feel about something we are passionate about. We shouldn't let anyone tell us, or try to tell us what our passions can be or how many we can have. I found two things I'm passionate about right now.

PASSION FOR WRITING

As I grew up and learned more about myself, I discovered my passion for writing. I found my purpose in 6th grade when my science teacher had us listen to a video by T.D Jakes "Run for your Destiny". And still to this day I can recite every word from memory, in that video. After she showed us that video, I went home and listened to it over and over. I listened to a couple of his other videos but then I started writing speeches of my own and recording them on my phone which I still do to this day. I have listened to so many motivational speakers such as Eric Thomas, Les Brown, and Kobe Bryant and many more. I would often stay up all night writing speeches because it was the only way for me to get away from all the negativity that was going on in my life at the time.

GIRL DRAMA

Many girls experience drama with other girls throughout their adolescent years. I remember in 7th grade I would pretend to be sick so that I did not have to interact with all the negativity. And it caused me to miss a qualifying meet to continue my track season that year. I did not want to lose love for something I used to escape the world because I was constantly surrounded by negativity. I almost lost one of the only things I found peace doing. I couldn't escape to my happy place anymore during the practices and track meets. Going back to what I said above, learning how to not let anyone get between you and your goals for your life is very important. My track season was cut short because I wasn't mentally ready to stand up to them. Going through this experience in my life taught me to never let other people disrupt my dreams, and that I can overcome anything life throws my way as long as I work through it and not let it take control.

It's crazy when I look back on my life. I knew most of those kids who were bullying me for the majority of my life. I had been going to school with many of them since kindergarten. I can laugh at it now because girls love tearing each other up for any and every little thing to make themselves feel better. With girls it's deeper, it's more about how they can get to another girl mentally and the hatred is relentless.

It's already hard not having anyone in your class who looked like you. On top of that I was always compared to the only other black girl in my class when I finally wasn't the only one. Deep down what hurt the most was I truly just wanted to be her friend. She was the only person who looked just like me. I wasn't 'just' "bullied" by her. It was a group of people who would do it through social media and iMessage, when I was at school and when I went home at the end of the day, it was like I couldn't escape it. It tore me down and took me to a dark place that I was only able to get out of because I made a choice to get help and find a way to escape the negativity. Writing speeches allowed me to see that I was letting this control and reduce my power in pursuing my dreams and goals.

I believe that God only puts you through things you can handle and he always has a reason. The next year another girl in the grade below me got bullied and because I had already gone through it I was able to help her through it and create a friendship. Girls don't just try to break you down physically they will do it mentally too, which I believe hurts a lot more. Finding girl friends that we can truly trust is difficult because sadly not everyone wants to see us win and jealousy tends to be the downfall in girl friendships.

The YOUNGEST

In 8th grade I started finding out more about who I was. I took track more seriously and I became more self-focused with my life. In track I placed 10th in the valley in the hundred meter dash. I was the youngest out of the top ten, and my freshman year times I would have taken first at valleys that following year. I always liked competing against older people; it gave me something more to work for. After I graduated from Carden, I kinda fooled everyone around me into thinking that I was in a rush to leave, that I had not even begun to mentally prepare myself for what was about to come. I had never gone to another school before. I had been there my whole life. As I moved onto high school I realized a lot was about to change. Carden prepared me academically for high school but little did I know God was preparing me for the next phase in my journey.

Although I didn't show it, I was terrified to go to a new school, especially high school. This new place was huge and I was a little person going to a place with way more people than I had been used to. Mind you, my 8th grade class had 12 students. I mean it's not like I didn't know anyone because I knew a couple of the other black girls from my track club experience. Regardless, life was about to get real messy.

TRANSITION TO HIGH SCHOOL

When I transitioned to high school I went from a whole bunch of white kids, to a whole bunch of black kids, the environment really changed. The way people talked and acted changed and I adjusted to a different environment as I moved from one to another. I remember at my new high school, I was often called white-washed in my freshman year by other black kids even though they could clearly see that the color of my skin was brown. They called me white-washed because of the way I talked and where I lived and because of how I grew up.

White-washed is a stupid term because white people are not the only people allowed to use "proper" English. Just because someone lives in the suburbs does not make them any-less black. As time went on it began to bother me more and I found myself changing the way I talked just to stop hearing that stupid term. I had to grow thicker skin as I soon realized some of these people weren't going to stop until they had nothing else to break down. I learned, the hard way, that you can't trust people. This was after finding my way into a very toxic friendship for two in a half years. I was often judged by the people I thought were my friends and I realized that if I didn't start thinking seriously about my life, I would be another nobody hanging around with a bunch of nobodies.

I also want to add that my parents' successes were often used against me even to this very day. I am adding this part in my book while I am in college because I feel like it is very important to get this off my chest. My parents' success has helped me see big things are possible but it has not given me a free ticket to success. I am working my butt off everyday to get to where I want to be in life just like a lot of you are. I tell people when they first meet me I have two successful parents but I want to be known for my successes and not my parents. I feel like penalizing and discrediting someone because of their background is wrong. That is a big reason I wrote this book to start building a foundation and a distinction between who I am and what I have to offer to this world. But let's get back to my life in high school.

My sophomore year in high school was not challenging educationally but the toxic friendship challenged me emotionally. My grades suffered tremendously that year as I tried to be friends with someone, who in the end was just using me. I was so focused on trying to make everyone else happy that in doing that I was coming closer to my breaking point.

I learned that it's okay to stop being friends with someone if they aren't adding or doing anything to improve my life. Realizing that made it okay to finally let go plus I was tired I just did not have anymore energy. I also learned it was okay for me to be my only friend because nobody's got me like I got myself. I challenge all of us to "WAKE UP" and become self-focused with our lives. The best thing I ever did for myself was to become self-determined with my life because not only were these people breaking me down emotionally, physically, and spiritually they were beginning to affect my goals I had set for my life.

But it took **me** a really long time to realize this, the key word is me, because whenever you are going through something toxic no one else can tell you to "let go," you have to realize it on your own. I refuse to let anyone drag me down with them when clearly I have so much to offer. I don't know how God does it but I thank him for bringing me through that so my story can help someone else. Although I felt very alone during that period of time and it was probably one of the lowest points in my life, I reached a turning point because of that experience and now I am a stronger individual because of it. Instead of letting that pain break me, I learned to use that pain as fuel to rebuild my life.

Keep in mind what I said: God always has a reason for everything he puts us through. Unlike in middle school I was able to use the pain I was going through as fuel. I trained harder,

I cried a lot; however, I didn't let what I was going through affect my goals, this time around. My sophomore track season was one of the best seasons I have ever had. I had finally broken 13 secs in the 100 meters and PR'd that year in both the 100 and 200.

HEADED TO AUSTRALIA

In the summer of 2019, I was invited to run at a track meet for the USA in Australia. I was trained by one of the best, gold medal olympic athlete Alice Brown, another mentor and guide in my life. I also got to experience the UCLA track program, after attending a UCLA track camp right before leaving to compete in Australia. I fell in love with the UCLA program because I didn't just feel like a teammate there but I felt like part of a family. Everything I had worked so hard for years finally seemed to be paying off.

After my UCLA summer track program in June 2019, I traveled all the way to Australia to compete in Track and Field Meet. I competed with athletes from everywhere in the USA and people from all over the world. You're probably thinking: "you went all that way to Australia to run for less than 1 minute". Hey that's the thing track athletes do, just imagine training all those hours for less than a minute. Anyways, I got to travel with my father, who has always been there for me since day one. The flight to Australia was 15 hours long and sadly I chose not to go to the restroom the whole flight and because of that I got a bladder infection right before my main event. Although that situation also sucked, the things I experienced during that trip were absolutely unforgettable. I also learned to never hold your bladder for 15 hours straight!

The memories and friendships I made will last a lifetime. Because of the bladder infection my times suffered in the 100 and 200 semi finals. But after the medicine finally started working on the last day I competed in the 4x100 relay for the USA team and we placed 2nd overall. I was the first leg and damn, it sure felt good to be back. My relay team and I also had become a family. It's crazy how close we got in that short amount of time. I know if I called Eryn, Jada, or Makayla for anything, they would have my back no matter what. Those girls are the definition of true friends. Although we all live in different states we still support and communicate with each other all the time. The beaches in Australia were breathtaking and if I have the chance to go again I would take it. That trip changed my life and it also made me a stronger person.

GLOBAL PANDEMIC

During my junior year in high school, I pretty much stayed to myself. I started distancing myself from everyone in order to find myself. I knew that I didn't have time for any more "F"-ups. I was getting good grades and became laser focused on my goals. This was my year and I had to prove myself. I was on track to run an 11.8 sec 100 meter. I was working my butt off at every practice AND BOOM, in March 2020 everything changed. Everything started to shut down due to the COVID pandemic. All of the schools shut down, all of the spring sports programs were canceled. Sadly, because of COVID I was not going to have my junior-year track season, the most important year in my track career.

As the quarantine kept extending, I again began losing myself. I remembered this one moment during quarantine, I felt like my biggest nightmare was coming true. I kept telling myself that without track I was nothing. I had lost the most important year for all track athletes, it felt like the world was really over. And there was nothing I could do about it. Deep down the thing I fear the most is becoming a failure, having all these big dreams I constantly talked about and then boom I don't achieve anything. Failing is ok and I know that but I feel like if I stopped at something before I have given everything I had that's how you become a failure. I had no control and I felt helpless. I had been down before but have never felt like this at all. However what I did not realize was that I did have control, I just had to make the decision to take it.

Still, I always kept in mind what I am capable of but as quarantine just kept going on and on, I began to see my whole life flashing before my eyes and it did not look like the vision I had created for my life. I was waking up and I wasn't motivated to do anything for a good 6 weeks. For the first time in my life, I was seeing my worst nightmare coming true. In that very moment, I felt like everything I had worked so hard for was lost. Nothing I was doing was working and I didn't know what to do, until I looked in the mirror one day. I asked myself, "Am I really going to give up and let COVID decide my future and control my life?" and "Is this really who Jasmine Phipps has become?"

Then, I remembered that I am someone who never gives up. But this did feel different, I actually briefly felt, for the first time, like I might not have any fight left in me. If we look deep enough everyone has a fight left in them, and we sometimes have to go much deeper to find it. So I did what I had done with past challenges, I started writing my feelings down, leading me to writing this book to inspire people my age to continue to fight. What's going on right now with the pandemic sucks but we can all choose to make our lives better. I now know for a fact that nothing life throws at me can stop me from achieving my dreams.

I choose to fight by taking a negative situation and turning it into a positive one. Not just for me but also to show my generation we can do anything we put our minds to. Everyone lost something during this pandemic and many people also lost themselves in the process. I found there is something inside of me that won't let me give up no matter what life throws at me. My mom told me my greatest skill is perseverance. When times get hard, I always decide to find ways to pick myself back up. I learned at a young age that no matter what, I can never let challenges, failures or setbacks affect my overall life goals.

In life, things do not always go as we may plan, but we can choose to do nothing or we can find our way back to chasing our dreams. COVID reminded me why I needed to succeed which gave me strength. As you read earlier, life has tested me before but never like this, it required me to use everything inside me to push forward to win this battle and continue to focus on making my dreams a reality. In this crazy moment in time, I truly found myself. Everyone of us will have life changing moments, when we all have our moment we must act on it. Everything I had gone through in the past, set me up to face what happened during the COVID pandemic but the pandemic set me up to face my senior year.

MY MESSAGE TO THIS GENERATION

The world tells us money is the answer to all our problems but is it really the answer? How can it be the answer to all our problems because in reality it can't provide us with everything the world has to offer. Even the richest people alive will never be able to buy more time. Time is one of the most valuable things in this world. Although it seems like we have so much time as young people, we really only have a finite amount. Time is valuable and we need to use it wisely. Ultimately, everyone's goal should be to maximize happiness since money can't buy it. For many people money is just a temporary solution because it is often fleeting. Money can't buy emotions, it can only buy material things. It is a temporary solution that leads us into temporary fixes, ultimately getting us nowhere but behind.

In my opinion, one of the biggest problems facing my generation involves fixing our long-term issues with temporary solutions. For example when we choose to get high we do it to try to escape from our problems, right? But we are only able to escape when we choose to be high. What about the times when we aren't high? My question is why? Trying to solve problems with something temporary only leads to us going back to temporary relief. They cause an endless feedback loop of running in and out of the same wrong door, instead of opening the door to permanent solutions to our problems.

As young people we are in a rush to grow up. Not many of us stop and think about what we truly want our futures to look like. I mean even as young children we can and should start asking ourselves what we want to be when we grow up. That question can come up as young as age 5, even if our answers change as we get older and have more experiences. Many young people can answer the question about what they want to be, but if you ask why, their answer will often have something to do with making a certain amount of money. The problem with living our whole lives chasing money, is that we may end up settling for a job or career that has nothing to do with our passion. God gives everyone talent and skills to be happy and money is not always the answer. We have to seek our passions first and often, eventually financial success follows.

Many people in our generation feel like we're mindlessly wasting our lives away because we probably haven't found our purpose yet. However, you find your purpose when you are ready and it may not be at the same time as the people around you. Everyone's purpose is actually often sealed before we are even born but we must figure out both how to unlock it and follow it. So many people let their talents go untouched because they get blinded by money or fear. Those two things often lead people to settle with what they are given, never asking for more. Elon Musk says, "Drive overcomes fear". I have been told,"Closed mouths don't get fed". If we don't ask for more outta life, we won't get more, it really is just that simple.

So we must not get stuck in a job we hate, and end up staying there, because we need the money. We must find something we love doing and the universal promise of life says that the money will follow. Finding something we are passionate about involves asking the right questions. So if we aren't happy with our lives we must change it. We need to spend time asking ourselves: deep down, what is it we really want out of life? Answering these important questions creates pathways for everything we dream to come true. We can't let our dreams die before we plant them in good soil and grow them into our futures. We can not let our fears stop us or block us from accomplishing our goals.

"The graveyard is the richest place on earth, because it is here that you will find all the hopes and dreams that were never fulfilled, the books that were never written, the songs that were never sung, the inventions that were never shared, the cures that were never discovered, all because someone was too afraid to take that first step, keep with the problem, or determined to carry out their dream."- Les Brown

Some of the wealthiest people started out with nothing but found their passion and put their passion to work leading them to their success. For example, Tyler Perry queried, "Why deprive the world of your many talents by only showing them a minor one[?]" What do you want out of life?

Passion leads us to our purpose which leads us to get paid.

PASSION -> PURPOSE -> PAID

The Vision

The vision starts with an idea which can come in many forms, such as a goal or a dream that you may have, or a thought you formed in your mind. Everyone has a vision of how they want their lives to be and in order to bring it to life, we use our passions to lead us in the right direction.

A passion is something you will do for free but people pay to see and it many times will lead you right to your purpose

Passions can change but our purpose in life remains the same. For example, each year we may create new goals for ourselves. Although we have new goals there is always one thing that in achieving those goals, helps us get closer to our ultimate goal and better know our purpose. Passions guide us to our purpose. So the first question is what are some things you like? It can help to stop here and write some things you like to do.

THINGS YOU LIKE (for example: I like to write)

1.
2.
3.
4.
5.

Now think about something you want to achieve this year? Why do you need to achieve them? Answering the "Why" part of the question is very important because you need to understand why you want something, to get it. When your brain understands why you need it, you are prone to do everything it takes to achieve it.

THINGS I WANT TO ACHIEVE

1.
2.
3.
4.
5.

WHY I WANT TO ACHIEVE MY LISTS

1.
2.
3.
4.
5.

Anything we can imagine is achievable, so whatever we want out of life is possible. Because we are young we have the opportunity to do anything we want with our lives. Our young age allows for the freedom to seek and find out what truly excites us. Our purpose often answers the question of why God put us on this earth. Let me break our lives down really quickly, God gives everyone including young people a purpose! Our lives are to be grown to the fullest, all we have to do is find the seeds (our passions) and plant them in rich fertile soil. In order for a seed to grow, it must be nurtured.

As the seeds get the nutrition needed, growth occurs. So as we grow our passions and water them through positive thoughts, vision boards, guidance and mentorship, we will begin to develop into the people we are meant to be. The resources lie within each one of us. We must use all of the resources we have to fulfill our dreams. If you haven't found your seeds yet, start writing about what excites you and drives you that will help define your passion. Our passion leads us right to our purpose.

Passion often comes naturally, passion cannot be forced and it's something that makes us intrinsically happy. Passion turns into that unexplainable feeling we have for something, it may keep us up at night. It may also wake us up in the morning. We normally keep doing it, no matter how hard things get. We can lose track of time when we are doing something we are passionate about. It is also something we never lose love for, and we never feel like we are being made to do it because we want to do it. Passion involves us wanting to spend time in the doing. Although passion fills us with happiness and joy, it still requires work.

Remember when we find our true passion, we unlock our true purpose. When we find our true purpose we discover who we are and what we want out of life. Our lives become clearer and that leads us to achieve everything we are here to do. Passion and purpose leads to our vision. The vision begins the journey to everything we want and helps develop the road map to our success.

Next question: what do you envision for your life? For example, my vision is to inspire not only my community but the whole world and show girls they have everything it takes to be successful. I want to motivate young women because I don't really see enough motivation like this in our world. At a young age I began working on an organization called, "Girls with Success" but I didn't really understand what to do with it until recently. More than ever young women and girls need something to build themselves up because so often we are torn down in this world. We are often seen as objects instead of humans. Every young woman has a purpose but many don't even get a chance to find it due to the many lies this world places in our minds. The lies begin to cause many of us to doubt ourselves before we even get a chance to find and map the road to our success.

How I Found My Vision

It is unusual for someone as young as me to want to be a motivational speaker . "How could I be a motivational speaker when I am so young? In order for me to be able to motivate others I would have to have achieved something by "going through things myself". However, as you have read in the beginning of the book, I have gone through many obstacles to get where I am today. I feel as teenagers we face tough battles and challenging situations all the time. We often make quick and not well thought out decisions that impact our lives forever but we still go through things. When I faced my many personal challenges and trials- including bullying, peer pressure and "girl issues- I looked to the adults in my life for help, guidance, and direction. However, I often wanted advice from someone my own age or even a little bit older than me. Someone maybe like me, who has gone through the same things I was going through at the time.

JASMINE'S VISION

It was through facing those challenges that I decided I wanted to be that voice for young women now. Growing up in today's world we can't only be educated in school. We also need to be educated on how to make our dreams become realities and on how to find our vision to take us into our best lives, as we grow up.

How to Find Your Vision

3 Questions to Ask Yourself

Question #1: What do you want out of life or what do you envision for your life?

As teenagers, growing up in this world, adults are always telling us how to live our lives. As we go through high school everyone asks us where we are going next? Everyone has a different definition of success, all of our success stories will be different. Start by sitting quietly with a pen and paper to write down: your dream job, place to live, car, house, and family life. The key to figuring out our vision all starts with our dreams and I want us to dream big! Only we know the answer to what's in our dreams. Don't let negative thoughts deny our abilities and affect the vision of who we want to be. Fear and negativity only limit our possibilities–the sky really is the limit but we must believe it to achieve it! Remember, because someone said I want to fly like the birds in the sky,we have planes today.

Question #2: What steps are needed to accomplish my dreams?

What education do I need for my dream job? How can I get that dream house in that dream city? With each question you write down answers that create the pathway to making your vision a reality in other words bringing it to life. The list needs to include everything we want out of life, all of it! It is key to remember that success has no price tag, nor any age limit. We may only know one or two things right now, but it only takes one block to build on another block. Start with one building block and we can build on top of it as more ideas flow. Freeing our minds allows our ideas to run over without walls, ceilings, or roadblocks. Finding our purpose will require us to dig deep and ask questions only we can answer. Everyone's purpose sits in a little room in our minds and all we have to do is open the door to our mind's eye to clearly see it. We also have to be willing to find it. Many of us haven't even scratched the surface of what we are capable of achieving. Achievement comes when we follow the road we map through our vision. (Read that twice if you didn't get it the first time.) We have the skills and all we need are the right tools.

Question #3: What do you do with the answers to your questions?

The answer is, actually, very simple: we have to create a plan because unless we have a plan our goals and our passions remain just dreams.

Everyone wants to be remembered somehow, so, what are you going to be remembered for? As I mentioned before many people die not ever knowing who they truly could have been. People die not ever even trying to find or follow their dreams. So now the questions we have to ask ourselves is who we are and what do we want out of life? Everyone is really here for a reason and this book is to help us all find our reason. For many of us it takes asking the questions that we have never asked ourselves before. So now take a minute to get up and go find a mirror. Look in the mirror and ask yourself "What do I want out of life? Know that you may not be able to answer it right away and that's ok. But I hope by reading this book I get you thinking so you are able to answer that question and be confident about your answer.

Turning your goals into success requires you to make a step by step plan, to reach your destination. Once we have our visions, we must create a vision board, like many of the most successful people in the world. Using the answers to our visionary questions allows us to build our vision boards. The vision board is where things get really fun and exciting because the skies are the limit and we can allow our imaginations to roam free. We must pull pictures from magazines, websites, and articles that match our ideal car, place to live, dream college, job and so on. Then we begin to see ourselves moving into the visions on our board. And the key to success is consistency. Start with one thing on your vision board and build to two and so on. A vision board is a daily reminder of your goals because you don't want them to get lost in your everyday responsibilities.

Example Vision Board

Once we have our vision boards going, seeing our plans up on a board visually cements our purpose through pictures that we can see daily. It gives us more reasons to wake up and start our days. Waking up with a visual of where we see our lives going is powerful! Do we all see it now? We really are the keys to our success, everything is about us all starting now. It's okay to be self-focused when it comes to creating our visions. Once we figure out who we are, and what our purpose in life is, it frees us to build our dream futures. Some of us will find our purpose right away, while others may take their time; regardless, we can all make it easier starting with a vision board.

So I am ending this chapter, challenging all of us to start living the lives we want to live now and in the future by creating the vision of our dreams. That vision sets up the reality for them to come true. "Why wait - Be great!" Why not start our lives now, by figuring out who we are by asking the right questions and seeking the right answers and following the dreams we create for ourselves!

The Decision

Life is all about decisions. We can choose to continue living the life we were given or we can choose to change it through our self-defined visions. Whether we live our lives by the circumstances into which we are born or create the lives we want, is truly up to us. Most of us do not realize most of what we do and achieve in life starts with self-made decisions. No matter how bad someone else wants to see us succeed, the only thing that matters is whether or not we DECIDE to act on our passions. Anyone can say they want change, just like anyone can say they want to be successful. But in reality the people who are successful at changing their life circumstances are people who make moves and decide to do something about it.

In order to make any decision we have to find out why it's important to us. For example, again, we must ask ourselves: what does success mean to us? Everyone's definition of success is different and the level of success we all achieve will not be the same either. Going to college, getting a job, or buying a house can be success for some; while for others it will be owning a multi-million dollar business and for others it could be running a nonprofit or community organizing, but it will be the type of success we were built for.

Our success, in the end, is truly our decision. If we aren't living the life we want to live it can be because we haven't decided the life we want to have. We may have already decided we are willing to settle for the life given to us through the circumstances we were born into. Hey! I am trying to tell you, our families do not have to determine who we become. We can change family trends and set new paths for future generations by being the first to go to college or the first to own a business or the first to become financially independent.

We must determine our dreams and goals so one day we are not disappointed and angry because we got caught up in a static family legacy. Legacies are changed by the first person in the family who decides to set out on another path. We must seek to live the life we want, not the lives our family has or the lives the world sees for us. So again I will ask, what do you want out of life? We can now double back and look at our vision boards because we have decided to ask ourselves the right questions and answer with our visions.

Know this, many people go through their whole lives settling with what the world gives them, but all they had to do was ask for more and they could've had more. The other crazy thing about us humans is often our favorite thing to do is to consume whether it's through media or through Amazon or through something else. Imagine if everyone was just consumers and there were no producers, our lives would fall apart, the world would fall apart. Part of my challenge to my generation is for us to become producers and not just consumers. Part of us becoming producers is us creating the life we want to live.

If we don't have plans when we wake up each day then we are just living day by day and waiting to see what the world has in store for us. Imagine if everyone lived their life like that, nothing would get done nor be created. If we are living our lives day by day now, then we are settling for what the world throws at us. This book sets out to challenge each one of us to stop settling with the bare minimum and instead ask for our personal best.

Living without a purpose, lets the minutes, hours and days go by that we can never get back. Remember time is valuable, and should not be wasted on the world's random patterns. Time keeps going but we have the opportunity to use our time wisely by setting goals for our lives. Everyone wakes up with the same amount of hours in a day just like everyone is given the choice about what they do with them. The reason I know everyone can be successful is because it's a yes or no answer. We either want to be successful or we don't know how to be successful or we may not even know that success is an option. I am here to say, and there is no beating around the bush, success is a choice! How we define success is a choice. And success is the best choice we can make for our lives. Taking time to choose what we want out of life is the key to our success. Then we must follow the steps leading us to the places we want to go. We can all choose this and choose it now!

At our age we are given time to figure out how we want to live our lives. We don't have any excuses. Many people get caught up in what they are going through, maybe it's a relationship with a guy or a messed up friendship with a girl and often those situations decide what happens in someone's life. Even something as challenging as that does not have to stop someone from achieving their dreams. What I am saying is, that it may be a detour on your journey but you can also look at it as a motivator to become even more successful!

Then you can teach your child how to dream one day and use their challenges to create triumphs. I'm trying to say that, we must stop putting stuff off, and stop letting what we go through control or define our lives. When we have a plan, it can often lead us to make better decisions about how to achieve the future we want.

Those challenges and detours can cause pain and disappointment but with pain comes strength and everything we go through can make us stronger. Every failure, every challenge, every detour is a lesson on our road to success. We can take control of our lives by making the decision to do so at any time. But I will remind you again, what we do with the time we have, matters! A lot of teenagers become consumed by social media, participating in drama and focusing on stuff that will not matter in the big picture of our lives.

A large part of growing up requires us to realize that eventually we are going to be adults with adult responsibilities. So if we spend a lot of our time focused on little things we end up losing valuable time that we could have spent planning our futures. That wasted time often ends with regrets and us trying to fix the negative short term decisions we have made. Although we can grow from these things, it should remind us that what we do now matters, period!

I don't care what anyone says; we can be successful whether we are rich, poor, 8,12, 16, 26, black, or white– success doesn't care about any of those things. Success sticks around as long as we are willing to fight for it. No one succeeds by accident as success is intentional. It doesn't matter what we are going through right now, everyone is capable of overcoming challenges and surpassing their wildest dreams, but only if we believe.

So if you are faced with a major life challenge or circumstance don't let what is happening in your life hold you back from making the decision to go on and succeed anyway. Everything we go through has purpose in our lives, God has reasons but it is up to us to turn those negatives and challenges into positive success. The question remains: What kind of life are we going to live from now on and are we willing to fight for your dreams?

After we decide to go for it, we must take the next step. My seven steps to success start with finding our passion and purpose which comes with the vision. After we find our vision, we decide how to bring it to life or we can settle with it remaining a vision. After all the work we've put in coming up with the vision, it would be a shame to let it go to waste. After choosing to bring it to life, our excitement can only grow as we begin to see what we can do with it.

Things we must remember along the way include: being okay with change, challenges and even detours along the way because after all, life is all about change. Also keep in mind that change may include dilemmas, such as, giving up a toxic friend group or not going to that party so that you can study to get an A on that test coming up. It involves changing the negative views we think about ourselves. It may involve changing the mindset of our families, who may not be used to us having a vision. We may have to be okay with being alone sometimes because the journey to success can often be lonely but in the end it will all be worth it. For if we really want to be great at something, we must be willing to do everything in our power until we achieve it.

Success vs. Failure

Believe it or not, failure is often a key principle to what makes people successful. Failure challenges us to learn new ways of doing things. Any failure can be turned into a success if we change how we think about it. Many people fall, get up, dust themselves off and then go on to succeed in huge ways. Some of the most successful people in this world have suffered many failures. For example, many people don't realize Michael Jordan did not make the varsity basketball team his sophomore year in high school but he used that as a catalyst for great success. Tyler Perry, was homeless for years while creating the character Madea who became a vehicle for his success, he is now on Forbes list of billionaires. Tiffany Haddish, became a successful comedian after growing up in foster care because she did not let the circumstances of her young life decide the course of her success. Oprah Winfrey did not let the fact that there were no talk show hosts that looked like her stop her from pursuing her dream and she never let her failures block her path to success.

If we let failure define us, we may regret letting it stop us from being who we are supposed to be. We must see that failure often doesn't happen from just one thing; failure can arise from a whole bunch of little problems that add up to a major issue or road block. When a driver comes up on a road block the driver must learn the detour, there is always a way around, through or even over a failure. We have to be willing to see the lesson in our mistakes and never hide them but take the good from that negative experience and do not let failure define us or stop us on our journey. Learning from failure starts with fixing little things that led up to the failure. Looking at how we got to that roadblock: did we not follow our own map for success, were we trying to follow someone else's vision because they seemed to be successful, or were we not following our intuition about a particular situation. It comes down to a matter of mastering the little things and the little challenges life throws our way while not letting them knock us down permanently.

This often involves us asking for help during times we find ourselves in trouble and not letting pride hold us back from admitting we made a mistake. Some of the most successful people know that they need help and don't hesitate to get help when roadblocks appear. Some successful people are born into their success and seem to be lucky, but for many who are born into success they still have to learn how to maintain it. We can use real life examples to build our dreams for success. However Success often becomes how we see failure and how we use failure to stop us or motivate us to go for more.

Success occurs when we learn from our mistakes and grow. In my journey many people would look at my ADHD as a weakness, but I looked at it as a strength and a challenge I could use to my advantage. Because of my ADHD I am able to focus on one thing and hone in on the task that I want to accomplish. Another challenge I faced was through being around people who did not have the same mindset for success. I found out in real time we become like the friends we keep. If I wanted to be successful, I had to change my friend set and even had to learn how to be strong standing on my own. Negative people create negative circumstances which lead to negative outcomes. This is where decision making becomes important-I always felt in my gut when things were not right but I did not always listen to my gut.

I learned that gut feeling was the voice of my intuition speaking to me, nudging me, reminding me that something was wrong. The lesson is to listen, we all get those feelings and know when things don't feel right. I am urging all of us to listen to our gut instincts. When we get into ruts, the reason we often fall into failure is because doubt sneaks in. Doubt and fear can drown out our voice of reason and positivity only if we let them. Having a vision on a board can help us shut down our fears; being able to see and visualize our dreams daily can lighten up things when they seem dark.

"Doubt kills more dreams than failure ever will."(WHO) Doubt and fear are the biggest human emotions holding our generation back from finding success. One of the biggest battles we will come across on our journey for success is the battle between success vs. failure and the battle of our dreams winning over our fears and doubts. So many people are afraid of failing they never see the possibility of success. Fear of failing often blocks people's success because part of the process of succeeding includes a willingness to fail. Again I believe, everyone can succeed at something but many remain too scared to even try just because they fear failure. Not trying often leads to a life filled with both failure and regret. I would rather fail than never try at something that could be the best decision of my life.

I want us all to know it's ok to start our journeys with a little fear and even some doubt. But more than that I am saying we must not let fear and doubt define our journeys. We can look at them as tools to make our journeys richer. We must challenge ourselves to face our biggest fears and doubts to see how to defeat them. No one wins every battle, we've all heard the saying, "you lose some and you win some, but it's how you play the game". If we aren't even willing to get in the game then we have already failed. Failure alone will cause us to miss out on the opportunities of our lives. If we never start something because we are scared to fail or we stop doing something because we have failed once, then failure becomes the final experience. So then failure invades our journeys and becomes cyclical, so we let our dreams die. Is it because the dream was not worth fighting for in the first place? One thing many people do not realize is that without ever trying something, you fail in the quickest way humanly possible.

The reason people become successful has always been because they didn't stop after failing but they persevered through their failures. My mom constantly reminds me to use my super power of perseverance when I am facing the many challenges I have faced. Successful people keep fighting until they achieve the goals they set out to achieve no matter how many times they fail. If they fail, they just keep getting up. When they see a stop sign or detour in the road they make their way around it. Successful people do not let those things stop them from moving towards their passion. Honestly, I believe no battle even gets started until we have failed at least once. So remember, success and failure are often a package deal.

So now we know we have to be unafraid of failure because failure is one of the biggest and most rewarding ingredients of success. We can see failure for what it is, as it's just another word for a challenge to be overcome. This can help us let go of thoughts like: "If I fail I might not be able to get back up from it?" or "If I fail am I going to feel lost forever?". Now, change the word "fail" to "challenge". Repeat the questions: "If I am challenged will I be able to be challenged again?" We all face challenges at some point, so yes, we can face being challenged again. Okay what about "If I am challenged will I feel lost forever?" No, of course not. Challenges and fears are things to overcome, not to define us. I can tell you, during the COVID quarantine, I sat for hours thinking about how I felt when I failed. Sure, it's painful at first, but then I would start to get mad. I then would get that fighting spirit that reminds me I am not the sum of my failures. I kept in mind that my failures have often added up to many of my greatest successes. So none of us can let fear of failure or just plain fear itself control our lives.

I used to be afraid that, if I failed at the one thing I loved doing the most in this world, I would never be able to love myself the same. But as soon as I became fearless and accepted failure as a part of my success, I became willing to seek success in everything I wanted out of life. I believe there are three different ways this battle can go: the first way is letting fear win by letting it control and eat us alive. In this way we don't even actually see the battle at all because we don't even start. The first way is the quickest ticket to failure.

The second way we fail is when the battle starts, we give up in the middle of the challenge all because we think or believe we will not succeed. In this situation we let fear and doubt lead us to failure before we even fully give it a try.

Lastly, the third way is when we push through with our plan and we fail, and then we let fear and doubt shut our plans down. The most successful people realize that at this moment the battle isn't over yet but it has actually just begun. When we have passion for our dreams and goals in life, failure is not a detriment; instead it is just a stepping stone on the way to our success. If we let perceived failure stop us from achieving our dreams and goals we will end up with regret.

It is in those times we must pick up all the broken pieces and rebuild ourselves and try over again. That trying builds our armor which allows us to move onto the battle towards our dream life. The third way of failure can really be a challenge for us, I think, is the hardest one to go through. Because in the third way we can see the way we planned to do things and still fail. To succeed we must then find or look for a different way to achieve our goals. It is also the greatest path to strengthening our focus and making us come up with a stronger pathway to follow. So I will repeat it again, we must not let first failure and heartbreak discourage our outlooks on our future.

If we stick with it and continue to push towards our dreams, failure can actually strengthen our belief. We can achieve anything we dream. I know everyone reading this book is capable of achieving any and everything they want in this life. Although I wish my belief was enough, it isn't, it will take all of us believing in ourselves! By now you must see that success is a mindset; our brains are powerful and we must believe in our ability to succeed. It doesn't matter how hard we train for anything if we do not mentally believe we can do what we trained for then we will lose. But if we believe we will succeed, we will. It seems crazy and simple because it is that simple: our belief in ourselves is huge. Regardless, we must make the decision and choose the belief!

I know it may have crossed your mind because it has crossed mine, nobody wants to be the person who was born, lived, and died because there is much more to life than that. Living life without a purpose is not truly living at all. I feel blessed because I found my purpose in life at a very young age. For some it takes more time and that is ok, but it doesn't mean we have to wait for it to come to us since we can actually find it-whether that be in ourselves or through new experiences. The biggest mistake anyone can make is waiting for success to find them. Remember what I said earlier, waiting only gets us behind. To succeed we must be willing to seek out our passion, plan out our pathway, and take the journey to our dreams. Keeping in mind our greatest success could just be one failure or challenge away. Don't be scared, take a deep breath and just jump!

Bringing Your Vision to Life

Once we figure out our road map to success we must start writing our success stories. The different accomplishments and obstacles we have to overcome create the different chapters in our stories; as time passes our success story takes shape. As we write our stories it helps us to better understand who we are and what we are capable of.

In order to bring our vision to life, remember we must start with the right mindset. Because our brain controls everything we do, wanting a better life or wanting more isn't enough. We have to believe we need it and believe we can achieve it. The question is how to become the best versions of ourselves? "We don't decide our purpose, we decide whether or not we find it."

Without the right fuel a car can't start; therefore, we have to give our minds the right fuel to start our journeys. It starts with taking control of our minds through positive thoughts because to build anything, we need a strong foundation.

Build a strong foundation for living our desired life

1. Vision

Our vision starts with finding our passions in life, the things we do that excite us and energize us. Everyone has passions, dreams, and goals but often we don't know how to unlock them. We have to sit down and ask ourselves the questions that will define our passions. For example: what do I love doing? Is it writing, singing, math, science, art, or taking care of people? Is there any career that peaks my interest that would include the things I love to do?

This is how we start to find our passions by asking those questions.

Once we determine the one or two things we love to do then we can develop a plan to make it happen.

2. The Decision

We must ask ourselves: why are our goals important to us? In order to take control of our lives and raise our standards to fit with our goals. Controlling our minds involves some self-discipline especially in a world full of distractions including social media, gaming and other media platforms. We often must pull ourselves away from those distractions to focus on developing our true and best selves. Sitting down with only yourself to discover what your vision may be and making decisions accordingly.

3. Self-discipline

What is self-discipline? Many people think of discipline in general as punishment. It is something that we set in our minds to keep us going, keeping us on track, and keeping us in line. Self-discipline is the thing that gets us up and helps us start our days. Nobody has to tell us to do it, when we locate discipline from within. As young people there may be times, we need a little help to get started, and in those moments we need to turn to our support. Then once we get to the starting line, it's all about how we keep going. For me, once I get to the starting line nobody can beat my start! Self-discipline is what's going to get us all where we need to go. Know that without self discipline we won't even get started.

1. So let's get started!
2. Let's do the things we want to do!
3. Let's get stuff done!
4. Let's make progress!
5. Let's build habits!
6. Let's make a routine to get the work done!

4. Sacrifice

We will all have to sacrifice at times in our lives but following a plan may help relieve some of that (stress from) sacrifice. We might not be able to go to a certain dance or a school event because we have to study to get that A. We may have to sacrifice relationships with people who don't support our goals or help move us to be our better selves. We will often have to sacrifice time on social media, going to movies to build our dreams. We need to give up our negative thoughts and replace them with positive ones. When we go low in our minds we must stop in that moment and go to a positive high! When we achieve our success, the sacrifices will all be worth it. We can not let setbacks stop our forward movement.

5. Follow a Routine

Routines help us with life balance, and setting up life directions. Routines include waking up at the same time everyday; doing some light exercise to increase blood flow to your brain; eating a good nutritious breakfast for brain food; reviewing and meditating on our vision boards for a great start to each day. Then we move onto what is scheduled for the day, like school. We may have to wake up a little earlier to do our daily routines, but that fuel will often help us get our brains going in a very positive way. As students, we also need to include a set study routine to allow for our success in school. If problems or issues arise, we begin with fixing one thing at a time and build on each fix while making lists to address any areas of challenge or weaknesses. We must maximize our time and be very careful who we choose to hang around with or how we spend our days. It is key for us all to be very intentional.

6. Make a Vision Board

Since we will all have different success stories, our vision boards will be very individualized. Our vision boards help us to create our own special plans. Unless we have a plan, our goals remain prospective. Goals cannot develop into plans without step-by-step road maps to our unique destinations. After we create the plan we can start thinking about our realities more concretely. Everything we do or don't do can affect our goals and plans so we must be deliberate in defining the structure in our maps. Remember we must be number one in our minds, meaning we must be the priority, and we can not lose sight of our long term goals if we can see it on our vision boards. Distractions can and often will pull us away from taking care of ourselves and when that happens we return to our visions. We may also find that our goals change along the way as our plans develop because the planning process often makes clear our actual vision.

7. Getting Out of Your Comfort Zone

Everyone must be ready to challenge themselves to find out who and what they want to be in this world. Go for your dreams even if it seems scary. Do what is exciting, not what feels comfortable. Our comfort level will increase as our visions become more complete. Sometimes it is easier to fit into someone else's expectations than to be an individual in defining personal success. But it is important that we must do what we want and not what our parents, or our teachers or other important people in our lives want. But we can ask those people for advice in our decision process. Comfort comes with positivity! Comfort comes from getting to a place of peace with our choices.

***

Celebrate every Success and Achievement

no matter how Big or Small

***

Maybe we get all As or do really well on a project, we must stop and celebrate those moments. When we reach a certain place in our vision, take time to note it and enjoy each step of success along the way. On our busy days we are often too preoccupied to stop and celebrate or even just smile as we make good moves forward. We must also be intentional when stopping to note our achievements. We can add our grades to our vision boards, medals for sports events, and keep programs for our school performances. Seeing our successes up in our own lights will help give our brains that positive power to keep us going.

Celebrations fuel our fires to succeed

LIFE AS A SENIOR

I wasn't going to add this part of my life in the book because Lord knows I was supposed to publish this months ago. But without my senior year, this book would be incomplete in my eyes. This part is especially for my girls because toxic relationships are so common nowadays and getting over one can seem impossible. But let me tell you it is possible because I got over one myself. I was in a toxic relationship for a cool couple of months. I believe from February of 2020 until the beginning of March 2021. The lessons I learned, the pain I went through and the challenges I overcame are endless. I know how mentally draining it is to juggle the pain of loss and whatever else life throws at you. And if you are going through challenges right now, I just wanna say to take it one minute at a time.

It got so bad for me, I almost took my life because I did not want to wake up the next day still feeling the same pain. Wait, before I go on with my story I want to make something clear; I didn't almost take my life over a stupid relationship. It was because I was holding everything inside from grieving the death of someone I loved dearly, to handling an unexpected injury, to not knowing what my life was going to look like in the next couple of months. I had put it all in this little tiny box but at some point every box has to be opened. On February 24, 2021 I almost took my life, because I began to think all the pain was never gonna go away. I let all those painful events build up leading me to make a stupid decision. Then I realized just how precious I am and you are too. I also learned not everyone deserves a piece of you. I am so lucky to have best friends that helped me get through that stage in my life but more importantly a mother who has been by my side as a shoulder to cry on. When going through toxic relationships you often forget your worth and become so numb to the pain you feel incomplete without it. You begin thinking painful feelings are both normal and okay and that's why we often run back. They say love is a drug and to stay away from it. I remembered my mom telling me Love is not a feeling, it's an action and that has stuck with me ever since. As women we fight so many battles we can't keep count. Truly finding out how to love ourselves is so important, especially nowadays. I am only writing about this traumatic part of my life because I hope it will help someone else. You may feel like this portion of my life speaks to you; keep in mind the key is loving yourself and love is not and should not be painful. I just want to let you know I'm so proud of you, for staying and believing.

On February 24, I just remember being so tired of crying I thought that if I went into the shower and filled up the tub then my tears would blend into the bath water. What I failed to realize in that one moment, was taking my life would stop only my pain but it would cause pain for all my loved ones who I would leave behind in this world. Although depression sucks and for a while it feels like nothing will get better, don't let it make you question living. I sat in that tub for 3 minutes and I kept hearing a little tiny voice in the back of my head saying "get up," but finding the strength to do it came from thinking that my little sister was just across the hall. We share a bathroom and so she was going to be the first to find me. Thinking of her seeing me lifeless in the tub gave me the strength I needed to get up because she was also fighting depression too. When I finally got up, I laid on the floor curled up in a ball for an hour crying. I then got up again and got back in the tub this time but this time I didn't fill the bath up I just turned on the shower. Something kept trying to tell me you can’t let depression win but that voice was so quiet I could hardly hear it. Then I remember running to my room soaking wet because I got in with all my clothes on. These feelings are so hard to explain but I looked up suicide on my computer and it said suicide lasts forever but pain is only temporary. I quickly called my mom and she stayed on the phone with me. I remember that day like it was yesterday. My parents, as they have always done in the past, got me the help I needed. I am very fortunate to be able to see a psychologist but at first processing the whole situation was very hard let alone talking to someone about it. I had reached breaking points before but if it wasn’t for God I wouldn't have been able to get out of this deep hole I had dug for myself.

The following couple of weeks I had discovered I had tendinitis in my left knee and to sum that up I also lost my senior track season. On top of that, getting out of a toxic relationship is an emotional roller coaster. I learned so much about myself through experiencing that horrible relationship, so it was a gift in disguise. But what I didn't know was God was about to put someone new and very important in my life. Although the time we shared went by fast, I appreciate every moment I spent with that person. Lol I know this chapter is getting long but bare with me I'm almost done, I think. I went through the month of March which passed by so fast, I just remember physical therapy being an illuminating experience for me to slow down a little and to be happy and proud of the little wins. Although I did not have a track season, I was able to take some time and rediscover my love for track. I am still writing this and it's July,but if you asked me a couple months ago "Did I think I was gonna run track in college," my answer would have been no. But here I am training this summer because I found an opportunity to run track in college. Okay back to the interesting stuff, I got through March and April was approaching faster than ever. One day I was scrolling through instagram and I saw that my high school was going to have a prom. Boy was I happy. I ran around the house at 3:OO AM screaming "I'm going to have a prom" about 5 or 6 times. Basically it went like this: the first dress I tried on was the one I ended up getting. We only had 2 weeks to get everything situated. I wanted a date but the catch was I had to get someone from my school.

Now the story on how I got my prom date is for another day but let me just say, "who would've thought". Anyways the prom pictures really tell it all. We went to prom in a limo. We all looked so beautiful and I danced so hard I ripped my dress. But now for the serious stuff, College Decisions were approaching. I was blessed to get accepted to many different colleges and very fortunate to receive scholarships as well. Everyone secretly wanted me to go to Cal Poly because it was close to home and it checked off a lot of boxes for me. I'm going to let you guess the college I choose. OK, I'll give you a hint it's Cal Poly for me.

Although my senior year did not go as I expected. In the end I wouldn't have had it any other way. All the memories I made from Prom to Graduation, to the person I am today, kinda makes me think I should have made a separate book called *Senior Year*. But if I could leave you with anything from all that I have learned from my senior year. I would say don't give up, celebrate the little wins as well as the big ones and have a lot of fun along the way.

Clearly you see with everything I told you about my life I never have had one moment where I could ask Siri for directions to my next destination in life. Life is never gonna give you a perfect route to your given destination, it's not even gonna give you a starting point because it's up to you to figure out every point for your life.

They say after a breakup girls do the unthinkable. Two weeks after the breakup they have a downpayment on a house, a car, and get a job. I know a lot of times the unthinkable seems impossible but I can't stress this enough, use your pain as fuel, don't let anything you go through control the next 5 years of your life.

I know what I want out of life and I also now know for fact nothing can hold me back and I know I won't ever give up. Remember when we go negative we must stop and turn our thoughts and words positive. So I decided to follow my own advice and build my plan for success. But I also decided to share it with my generation so we can all achieve success.

Remember, if who we are hanging around is not contributing anything positive to our lives: then ask why hang out with them? The way I see it is, our lives are like seeds and our purpose comes from how much water and sunlight we give to our plants. When we finally grow into the beautiful flowers, plants or trees we want to be, then we will finally see our success. The seeds get watered as long as we keep putting in the work to accomplish our dreams and goals. The soil we plant our seeds in includes the friends we surround ourselves with; so if we hang around a whole bunch of weeds or "day by dayers" we will become those things. We need to hang around people who are going to contribute to us and our success or our seeds will die and we will have to continually replant new seeds.

I definitely wish someone would have told me earlier, that it's okay to be self-focused when it comes to accomplishing my goals and dreams. No one can take anything away from me but me. Some of us will have to replant our seeds a couple of times but that's okay as long as we keep getting up when we fall and keep trying to be champions of our lives.

What Next

I've been trying to write this chapter for a while, and I finally started because you are reading it. I don't know why but this has been one of the toughest chapters for me to write because up to this point I am still discovering answers to some of my questions for myself. When I look back to the beginning of quarantine I see myself very scared of what the future had in store for me. When I look at my future now I see a blank paper and pencil waiting for me to define it. Covid sucks! Yes but because of it I was able to learn so many things about myself, and I am proud of the person I am becoming. I still have tough days, just like I'm pretty sure you do as well. My life still feels like a roller coaster but I am not scared of the future because everyday I take it a step at a time to better define it in the way I want it to be.

So I ask, what's next?? You can take that question and whatever you come up with will be correct because you answered it for yourself. There is no right or wrong answer when you answer that question. Key word is you and it has been throughout this whole book. Success isn't how much money you get, or how much you get for your achievements, it's how you feel when you succeed.

You define success on your own. As you are still writing your own success story everyday, so am I. I just recently was able to answer many questions for myself. When I asked myself:

what's next, there were so many other questions that popped up in my head. For example, what's next after I finish this book? What's next after I graduate high school? What's next now that I've gotten into college? Although that does answer what's next in my life in general, it doesn't answer what's next right now. What's next for me is I'm going to work on becoming a better me. Achieving success is one thing, but when you help someone else achieve their own success it's an even bigger success for yourself.

Everyone this year lost a "normal" life as a teenager but we are still here today, and on top of that going to school everyday behind a screen, conquering something even our parents didn't have to go through themselves. This generation is teaching themselves self-determination because as much as we use technology, we still continue to find a way to integrate school onto it even though it can be draining. However when we open our computers everyday, and log on to whatever program we are using for school we are succeeding, but not only that we are showing hidden greatness because we haven't given up.

Although I made many positive comments about quarantine, I struggled with depression this year and I know I'm not the only one. There were many days I stayed in my room in the dark thinking: is all this going to pay off? In the long run I improved because I remembered what I have accomplished and nobody can take my successes away from me. I turned my thoughts around and I do it regularly as we are all still living with this pandemic.

It's like we are sitting in a never ending chain of homework and every time you get all the work done that was assigned they add more so even though you aren't procrastinating it feels like you are. You'd think because I have only three classes a day I have so much extra time on my hands but I don't because everything else that comes with being a teenager eats away at it. I just turned 17 in November 2020 and although I am not on my own yet in many ways I am teaching myself how to be. I grew up observing everything and that's why I think I am the way I am. Jasmine before quarantine and Jasmine now are two completely different people. I've grown in so many different ways and learned so many things that I wouldn't have been able to learn if it wasn't for the time quarantine allowed me to spend time with myself.

I started writing this, my first book at 16 and I'm now going to be a 17 year old author. I had a vision and it took me 6 years to learn how to bring it to life. I have always had a gift when it comes to talking about my many passions, but this passion not only felt different, it led me to my purpose. Over the years I have developed skills to help me further my gift. It takes 10,000 hours to master something and I found my gift when I was 11 and I am barely scratching the surface of my potential. My 11 year old self decided that she was going to change the world and I was serious, all the time, tears, and pain I have, I poured into this book. And to think it just took me saying I want to do this and I'm going to do it. Although I didn't know 6 years ago that I was going to end up writing a book, the only reason it was possible was because my vision was too bright to be dimmed. It's crazy when I read speeches that I made in 6th grade to the ones I write now, I have come a long way. All those nights I stayed up writing and recording made me the person I am today. I had a vision and I brought it to life because not only did I believe in myself but I made it happen by putting the work in. Everyone has their own success story they are writing, so now the question is: is it going to be worth reading in the end?

As much as I lost during quarantine, I have gained so much more but like I said it's all about the choices! If it wasn't for one day during quarantine that I decided enough was enough and I am going to make a positive out of this big negative. Well I wouldn't even be writing this book today. I was inspired by so many but like I said this last chapter has probably been the toughest to write because I didn't know how to start, but now it's done.

Now it's your turn to begin your story.

Made in the USA
Columbia, SC
30 January 2023